rushes from the river
disappointment

THE HUGH MACLENNAN POETRY SERIES

Editors: Allan Hepburn and Carolyn Smart

Titles in the series

Waterglass Jeffery Donaldson

All the God-Sized Fruit Shawna Lemay

Chess Pieces David Solway

Giving My Body to Science Rachel Rose

The Asparagus Feast S.P. Zitner

The Thin Smoke of the Heart Tim Bowling

What Really Matters Thomas O'Grady

A Dream of Sulphur Aurian Haller

Credo Carmine Starnino

Her Festival Clothes Mavis Jones

The Afterlife of Trees Brian Bartlett

Before We Had Words S.P. Zitner

Bamboo Church Ricardo Sternberg

Franklin's Passage David Solway

The Ishtar Gate Diana Brebner

Hurt Thyself Andrew Steinmetz

The Silver Palace Restaurant Mark Abley

Wet Apples, White Blood Naomi Guttman

Palilalia Jeffery Donaldson

Mosaic Orpheus Peter Dale Scott

Cast from Bells Suzanne Hancock

Blindfold John Mikhail Asfour

Particles Michael Penny

A Lovely Gutting Robin Durnford

The Little Yellow House Heather Simeney MacLeod

Wavelengths of Your Song Eleonore Schönmaier

But for Now Gordon Johnston

Some Dance Ricardo Sternberg

rushes from the river disappointment

stephanie roberts

McGill-Queen's University Press

Montreal & Kingston • London • Chicago

ISBN 978-0-2280-0167-6 (paper)
ISBN 978-0-2280-0301-4 (ePDF)
ISBN 978-0-2280-0302-1 (ePUB)

Legal deposit second quarter 2020
Bibliothèque nationale du Québec

Printed in Canada on acid-free paper that is 100% ancient forest free
(100% post-consumer recycled), processed chlorine free

We acknowledge the support of the Canada Council for the Arts.

Nous remercions le Conseil des arts du Canada de son soutien.

Library and Archives Canada Cataloguing in Publication

Title: Rushes from the river disappointment / Stephanie Roberts.

Names: Roberts, Stephanie, 1965– author.

Series: Hugh MacLennan poetry series.

Description: Series statement: The Hugh MacLennan poetry series

Identifiers: Canadiana (print) 20200192280 | Canadiana (eBOOK)
   20200192337 | ISBN 9780228001676 (paper) |
   ISBN 9780228003014 (ePDF) | ISBN 9780228003021 (ePUB)

Classification: LCC PS8635.O2276 R87 2020 | DDC C811/.6—dc23

This book was typeset by Marquis Interscript in 9.5/13 Sabon.

for The Unmet

CONTENTS

rushes from the river
disappointment

those of us who've seen miracles know how to ask.
if you've asked, *do you love me*, i almost certainly
don't love you. and if,
in a flu-ish bout of poor judgement,
i've asked likewise then,
like death and taxes, by now you've retired,
with fire, to your silent
battle station. be that as it is.

we agree without asking to say nothing about all this strident
confused unbelief – keeping our conversations
to the whether [sic] and that guy who can swallow
a rubik's cube through a mustard-coloured disaster of teeth
solving the puzzle of it (via revolting convolutions in gut)
before regurgitation. i bet that guy believes in *i love you*.
i bet that guy asks for anything he wants.

let her come, unbidden, her water creeping the basement feet
as wind critical of the steadfast white pine, sorrowing along
our shared fencing, will take electricity for ten days in the guts
of december, when blue-eyed frost pushes back against twenty-
first century certainty, cracking the foundations of the suburbs
like eggs, and then again (incredibly) two weeks into august,
after a republican forest of lightning transfers displaced ocean
from mystified sky, washing away forever the dreams
of a motorcyclist, at exit thirty-five off the twenty, and by the
fate
of a despondent maple fork sleeping sundered on power lines,
running through our stands of ash, behind the quiet misery
of homes in the crescent, from that storm, come and gone, we
(way up north) relearn the word *swelter*, which my body reined
by intermittent swims amid the cool horses of risen river.

let her come, is what the orgasmic dream says, rocking
desire with a picture of your rider, head thrown back,
teeth arcing darkness, like the waxing scimitar of moon,
staunch opposition to night's quake of thin navy gauze.
then you remember how much pressure it takes to know
amber flesh under cloth over bone. her eyes, nothing like
a wildcat's gold coldness, are a wildcat's intemperate
bloodlust. perspiration chains the heart's assurance
that you don't have the power to let her do anything.

THE WOODS OF PERHAPS

Maybe, you've grown exhausted
by the woodland white baneberry
that looks up and through you.

Willow, it is possible that cracked
by afterclap of lightning, you fall
into the fork of my branched wait.

Dare I yet machete a procedure
threading scrub underbrush to the floor
of a warm smile armed for melancholia.

Mayhap, the snow that froze atonement
for your birth has nestled
under sun-fired spring trillium surrender.

Are we frightened aspens, colonial black
and white, thread beneath worm-turned
earth, two only in appearance?

Baby, shy-blue moon fuelled mature
steam; you run from the forest magnet,
weather permitting, our shared adventure.

Perchance, one day you wake in a tub
of cold blood come warm. Then, will you let
this whole forest of hurt love you?

Would I sing of incorruptible grief
writ in our skins, cantata complicit
to your tears and my implausible joy.

Perhaps, slumped like yellow sprung lilies,
head on shoulder under longing's glaucous
shade, hands link, prickly children cling.

this drama hums birched, blue,
and pine behind winter-closed doors
where raccoons and rabbits still.

i remember the evening's autumn
cathedral when amber light
massed in prayer above. i played

over the under of your body.
don't think Nietzsche would be
angry because under

i explored this penumbra'd path
round a temporary pond jewelled
with drake and hen lusty

in spring swell – winter's death
finding level. finding its lever
opening to a love-tossed bed

lipped by the cold fast recede
of white mountain to the black
ocean south aching and taking.

each spring a hesitation.
                                    the surface
of lindens throb ebonized by rain

and the lime-gold glow of old
and future dangle folded as fresh
cicadas on bracelets of branches.

an owl will pass silent as a nightmare
from tree to memory as cadet-grey dusk
hues into prussian blue mystery.
from an ink basin of reckoning
a water bird gurgles a lunatic's cry.
whoever cannot sleep, like the screech,
may hunt the sinuous path of fallen
timber and stone cleared as conduit
through trembling wombs of cedar
to the revelation of the lake's pelvic girdle,
where night's subtle frequency rides
the path of linden on a stubborn breeze
to a far and luminous town
searching for the garrison
that annihilates solitude's
thirst. so many trees standing and gone.
so many and somehow never enough.
moon rises over a child's fantasy;
restive tongues sort love's misspelling.
your shape holds howl invisible
sharp pain – nested pheasant
– coagulate arousal our porcelain hours.
diaphanous flower crushed
in night's ambivalent talons,
the owl-hunger lights
her perch. she sees where you lost faith
in dreams and now lie to yourself,
ready to be eviscerated. hand death
to the dying so hunger and desire lean.

FATHER SON SPIRIT

even though
you are almost certain
there is no one at the end
of the receiving line
you scrunch eyes
and whimper
please

a single breath of despairing
to whatever sieve can tongue it
hammer claw it
bowl cup hope
defines you

here
you journeyed *deathmarch*
through jungle belief ... forgetting it
during monsoon season
your overturned conviction
in a father you always find
in the desert

staked as forsaken child
with your foot in a snare
lupine howls sing
faith
into thunderation
fully grasping the paradox

because pain *don't care*
what makes sense
ghost and alone
produces sad
animal scratching
noises

even if the only response
that will or won't
is the silent
coming up after the third light
fast on your left
on the corner
of saint this or that
of the holy order of here and there
of a kaleidoscope abyss
and what you name it.

in the morning, there is no day job
to be alarmed by, and my waking
hours toll same as yours.
black coffee, sweet jesus, and the
white toilet follows same as you.
dig six feet for the sleep of tulip
bulbs as the québécoise neighbour
plays that one soul mix she's so-
proud-of, singing, smoking grass,
and reckoning sam cooke's pain's
the same as hers.   in   cold
october, sweat weeps even as frost
fingers   under   my
clothes.
plant a spring dream for colour.
kiss before confinement and snow.
   françoise hangs over the fence
offering a toke. i'm not resigned nor
inclined to start sharing her
samenesses.
e v e r y w h i t e b o d y knows
everything. painting my nights
black and blue with grief then
copyrighting the music.

i was handcuffed! (paul outraged
with sky-eyes wide.) wrongfully
arrested and no job! you think i
don't know what it's like to be
black! imblackerthanyou.
i keep my white thoughts to myself
— *ain't nothing blacker than that.*
let them think i'm burying crocuses,
daffodils, and hyacinths — sunrises
and sunsets pastel approved, but i'm
putting white bodies in these holes
— digging deep, adding bloodmeal,
laughing about it to the righteous
earth.

You're not going to get details
of whose bedroom I was in,
no name no place,
if it was October when the shadow
of mountains fell on the alley
of misconduct, or
the date and gestation
of a stillborn funeral capped
in dark curled hair, not
what endurance of contempt
culminated in a tsunami,
on the laundry day of divorce,
nor the contours of
the viper-rotten swamp
of unrequited love
in which I trained
for the Olympics.

I dart like a knife
into the confectionary,
amid chocolate-covered cherries,
hidden filberts, pralined pecans,
and maple syrup lollipops,
(50% off post first of July)
all to avoid a face
at your height and hair.

Something about George Harrison
is ruined for me now,
like Father's Day always was.
Wedding announcements
bring me zero joy. Lustre gleams
as a private matter, a keepsake,
only worshipped
away from the scrutiny of storm clouds,
or unbothered in a bar
over handheld glow, bitter silver
recollection set to Andrew Hale
and corn whisky.
After Valentine's, flowers grace
trash bin vases;
the pharmacy carts
boxed hearts three quarters off.
And it's said
the mobile destroys us,
or so *The Atlantic* clucked
like Henny Penny. Sincere texts
or sentimental paper moves,
we halt in the light of dimming
fire, our mothers progressed
by revolver under pillow
or not at all.

The day after Halloween
is guillotine.
After the fame of misfortune, I/you/we
present thanks for our wine-sick
hearts, for our daily gluten,
place our hope across a line
to the triumph of mauve solitude.

BOOTS OF SPANISH LEATHER

Because you said the music of my sighs chime seraphic, i told the milkman
(in a tone so low he had to lean in to my punch & whisper) *i will have
your money for you monday.* he seemed pleased to leave sung upon
& unsatisfied, & i didn't stop conquering there – i believed in you like May

Because you pierced me as an angel of light falls dagger & yawning
from heaven, i thought i could gain knowledge of good & evil eating
every orange & purple verb move of your sweet black sentencing
(spreading butter-memory & honey-fantasy) – i hungered to a happy death

Because hope's stench fumes from the pocket of the heart's bottomless
fray, from head & entrails too, i almost fell in my weary want for eternity
– a you & me from before all, to end all. Before you, after, & certainly
at the time, i thought us all this & Bob Dylan too.

THE OPENING LITURGY OF THE MORNING'S FIRST DRAFT IS ALL FUCKING WHILE THE EVENING MAKES LOVE AS THE GOOD POET PUTS IT

ironically in the morning the soles of your feet
ache only after you've rested them in dreaming.
plantar fasciitis to companion the broken glass
strewn over the last inches of life toward the downer
of decrepitude.

across from these pessimistic manias, against
a duck down pillow, the summer peach of your
days breathes mortality's fragrance, from a landscape
known and beloved as coney island, and the years
(kind and not) folded and unfolded the flesh surface
to the jaw where this whole damn loveliness hinges
bello with the bloom of a semi-harvested field of stubble.
a stiff brush from a man's pain abrades the willing
path down an unclenched valley with sighs made of fire.

open your hymnals to sixteen ninety-one.

this is the other who is also the same – the one
whose eyes spark an amber intoxicant of attraction.
the spring river swollen and unfrozen tears through you
high and gasping – the x at hell's crossroad.
your grip on the rim of reason is mystery and your
shared blood-type, where no wrinkle nor darkness dare.

repeat after me. repeat after me.

you could twist all broken up over the grey,
white, cold, and always the coming november,
if you're fool enough to hoard the misery-coloured
days' subtractions instead of the violet flare of
this early hour's jazz and the melancholy measures
of ben wolfe and orrin evans. it raises the salt level
in the eyes, oh yes it does sisters, and now you decide
again to be grateful, praying to the sleeper beside you
(a known foolishness but thoughtful), thanking
him (your god!) for his very survival – just be! and
then comes the amen of the tips of god's waking,
first, middle, and third, fingers placed on your tongue
the preamble to prayer and the opening liturgy
of i love you.

i never tire of the moon

a low sliver, silver they say. so long & good-bye
against the growing violet felt, it seemed to

hurt the sky by twin fire of emphasis and opposition.
crescent, comma, scimitar, it was all of these things

& none. it was a seizure of the mind it was:
time travel, extra sensory perception, aliens,

god's fallen lash, and lucifer's lopsided smile flaming
down the night. i sent a prayer, *are you seeing this?*

thankfully, we share the same sky if little else.
ice shacks on a partially frozen river skirt

measured disaster. i wanted to run home along our
fault line, tell you all about it, like a bloodhound

retrieves a hare, lays it, noses the fork of your stance,
slobbers joy, hungry for my happiness.

SET FIRE TO STOP FIRE

my whole life i've
                    done with this
walked out
never to return mid

riot geared nightmares
night vision the hall
of my grandmother's

these feet won't pedal in reverse

i've evaded every reunion,
i can't miss an *ex* anything

honey not sour enough
black hide not thick enough
heart not cold enough to clasp
the broach of nostalgia

control burn letters
while i loved them
then couldn't ache for

what was forgotten

i don't know what
but something
and soon.
this is my first memory.

i'm going to write a book called *god awful poems*
comprised of the most red love poems
my sad glad mad heart can mustard.

mustard (the colour of sorrow's altitude),
what best befits the travesty of tube steak
not vile sweet tomato sauces.

something terrible isn't going to happen,
and the lies about love i believe in *ain't happenin'*
neither – no matter how much the poets sing.

i'm going to write a book called *a poet's gotta eat;*
it's going to have a poem about this couple sitting
across the aisle, touching each other religiously,

comprehensively kissing the hollows of their
hope, nuzzling the pulsing plains in their necks,
counting with lips the knuckles they will bruise,

all before one or the other goes to the washroom
to empty themselves. i will script this mist in a diabetic's
blood as the insoluble truth about love.

i'll sell you above your romanticism or cynicism.
you'll wander the earth wanting this terrible terrible
to strike you while little by little your heart

muscle withers when you hope love is happening
and it isn't.
you will remember your first memory.

you will be in the book of god-awful poems.

CATCHING SIGHT OF THE NIÑA THE PINTA AND THE SANTA MARIA

borrowing a phrase from Frank O'Hara

i can tell you i wasn't expecting
the apocalypse to come bearing a mizzenmast.

i almost remember when the razor kissed
bleeding the clouds holding gold daydreams

not shading the water as a broken branch
or bloated corpse facedown lips eaten by fish.

mermaiding the ocean green for viking silver
you caught sight of my wake signalling land;

hawking the radiant eviscerate blue for food
if only i'd known an arrow was glinting from the pinta,

illumine my ruby belly but what you want remains
mysterious – tugging your joints to water's end.

love's three exhausted bombs twitched in hunger
i could have told you my blood sates *nada*.

i'm going to be in love again

used to be the big department stores in the city
closed on sunday
those early morning trains belonged to
black church goers
copped to king james unaware
how rare they were
christmas day you could drive from wall street
to harlem a mile a minute
did it once (can't remember why)
maybe because i could
like i'm going to love again
in spite of this exhaustion of entropy
consuming my heart like cancer
(never met anyone with heart cancer
or i never met anyone without it)
can't close stores now
literally a done deal
i'm not on the F heading to the church
opposite carnegie hall
where i sang all four verses shoulder to shoulder
with a tenor from the met
i'm embarrassed to still be off-key
about love
talked about it ten years twenty
          (enough already)
let the workers go
home to their families

for fuck's sake
let's get sick of talk of love
let's threaten poets with physical harm
i'm going to love again so quietly
no one will know
i'm home.

COMMUTE THE SENTENCE

every day i experience thinness cracking to bits

along a line of recurring grief

a monochrome voice echoes continue

without end

last words' dissolute purple

smokes into scene

of nursery, middle school, trains

never arrived their station

mortality picks a blue thread a long way off

love fuel to ransom beauty

new yorkers bridge and tunnelling

more rodent than resident shroud

under bridges division.

his selling points include "fairly good shape"
liberal politics a breezy concept of god
   checklists presenting
   banged-up circles for easy handling.

into this desperate mechanics turns
the gears of hard consonants
hikes, bikes, kayaks, walks,
   toils of past-time that toll hollow.
   now you wish the goddess to flame
   on one immune to the sting of obsession.

couch as well static commiseration when

you ought to hew a ladder to moonlighting
   ought to winnow the ivory husk of lie
from the hard brown kernel of love
   ought to grind hips and courage for
a deliberate seduction
   ought to knead openly your salted tears
into the toothsome sustenance of thriving
   acquit yourself as a dark flame of hunger
and thirst not white impotence
   to be divided with "female same" in an
uncaring wasteland of north floridian tomb.
   è la caratteristica della saggezza di
non fare cose disperate.

THE PHYSICS OF LOVE AND OTHER UNCERTAIN
PHASES OF THE CHEMISTRY IN COULOMB'S LAW

I. The Faster You Move the Heavier You Get
(mass energy equivalence)

$$E = mc^2$$

Which made you want us to
slow
up
a
bit
to remain comfortably within
your carry-on baggage limit.
I murmur to this jackrabbitheart, s l o w d o w n; for you,
I will be lighter (tv, magazines, haircut and colour, social
media, the hydrogen of the sun), much less like flight (hawk
claw-dive at dove-retreat as hell-on-fire), and not blame the
universe (sitting high and mighty changing particles to waves
and waves to particles belly-laughing with tears over our
perplexity) for being speedy and giant.

II. The Greater the Distance the Less the Force of Attraction
(Newton's Law of Universal Gravitation)

$$F = G \, \frac{m_1 \times m_2}{d^2}$$

I straight up wasn't trying to sneak a hit past you with this
for instance. Didn't yet know how much I would suffer
how far you could go without moving. Here is the paradox
of comparing hairbrushes to hammers. The moon falls fugitive
to the earth, the earth to the sun, and I bent and broke over
the thieving moon. Physic and love resist the reconciliation
of their likeness adding, *Yes,* and *Oh god,* to the whatever-span
of our postal code.

III. The Faster You Move through Space the Slower
You Move through Time
(the Lorentz factor and time dilation)

$$T_A = \frac{T_B}{\sqrt{1 - \dfrac{v^2}{c^2}}}$$

And now, *time* cracks knuckles, tenses biceps, takes a few
quick
test
jabs,
and appears to complete the hoodoo of its voodoo.
Time? What is time with another star – another planetary
once over?
We drove from Maine to New Brunswick. We watched the
knowledge of satellites add an hour of our life in an instant.
We make it up, we go along. Perception was cobwebs thick
across the immortal night of forgetting; I did not linger in
them – having no other nature than Venus' hot-quick lust.
We moved from hot to cold (the only time that matters) then
back again. Rovelli believes the illusion of time is hurting our
thinking in physics. Time hurts as we pulse in tachycardic
and bradycardic vortices. Now, when you die it will seem to
take ages and ages; it will be hard for me to tell.

IV. Information Entering Black Holes Is Lost Forever
(second law of black hole mechanics Bekenstein-Hawking
entropy)

$$S= \frac{1}{4} \frac{c^3k}{Gh} A$$

This one is pretty. And uncertain. A prettier bit of mischief
I never did see. If I took hold of your lower jaw with my
smallest
fingers resting near your lobes and my thumbs lightly against
the the start of your *ah*, would I find where you seem to begin?
The universe rather than being mostly nothing seems to be
mostly
a real invisibility.
Why the dark matters.
Why I reclaim the beauty of Blackness.
Why the approach of the tongue of my hopes is drawn in by
your gravity.
Will hope be forsaken as age dismantles optimism?
Vanquished
in cooling, transformed into lost-to-us-forever?

V. The Tendency to Move from Order to Disorder
as Time Goes On
(Boltzmann's entropy formula)

$$S = k. \text{Log } W$$

Socrates believed we went from an order of complete
knowledge
to a mysterious disorder some point post-birth. Then, physics
and philosophy have gotten along from way back, as
subjectivity in the philosophical is prescient of relativity in
the physical.
But we
have
defied
entropy,
emerging (as we did) from a chemical panic of: wanting a
petal's touch, New Year's Eve dance, the competition of the
music of our *mistery*, the correct accent on our varying
shibboleths, the puff and posturing
of incompatible blues (yours being phthalo a naturalistic hue
with green and mine being ultramarine the one unbound).
Like windswept waxwings fucked-up on fermented
mountain ash fruit, we circled each other berry-stained
and out of our goddamn minds demanding, *Who are you!?*
Demand wretched with delight. As time punched
through layers of answering and walls of unanswered, an order
of hostility and contempt painted fabulously neat bird boxes
with razor wire and prison bars wherein bittersweet chaos was
wholly contained, and what says order quite like
incarceration?

VI. Opposite Charges Attract Similar Charges Repel
(Coulomb's Law, the theory of electromagnetism)

$$F = \frac{kq_1q_2}{d^2}$$

Chapter 1: Break and Enter

Three days after Snow Owl's birthday, on a morning
sunny but raining, she loosed herself from the old scrape
she was sick of and headed North, high and far on silent
beats till expire and exhaustion were her only friends.
There she saw Polar Bear.

From a posterior approach, Owl rested on his back
so quietly she did not alert him; there she slept.

Polar bears have panther skin and translucent hair.
It is a misunderstanding they deeply resent – being mistaken
for white. When you look for opposites they are suddenly
very hard to find.

Owls are not wise as much as they accurately intuit
the feelings of others and can see the future. Owl woke
between the bear's paws.

  "Are there good and evil beings?" Owl asked.
  "No, only the charming or tedious."
Owl liked Wilde also but parried,
  "There are only those we think we're better than
and ourselves."

Chapter 2: Carrying a Concealed Weapon.

When Hades yawned, Owl saw a chasm limned
with anarchy. Hades thought Owl smelled (with her
sweet pungency of pine needles and clear sap)
like his future wife or dinner.

"Hades, are you going to eat me?"

Hades was tired of questions. Hades could not make up
his mind.
"Anyway! I will love you to the end," Owl sighed
very annoyed.
"You have timeless eyes," Hades whispered. His anxious
smile fragrant with remnants of seal meat.

at 11:11, after an absence of months,
after lingering, as a pair of glowing
eyes in and around the mouth of the
submarine-grey tiresome of social
media, you emerge – the large
silvered wolf whose love and hatred of
life is still full of fangs.

ravenous, you eat the meat of attraction
maddened that curiosity and desire can
be contained in the shadow of a
profile. only under a contract of *no
privacy limits* will you stay demanding
her unarmed hand for frustrated: snarls,
kisses, or silence. the question is, who
cares? who cares who submit to
whom? take the credit, set the terms,
finger her photos, fake your future,
take her body of evidence, take, take,
take until all candyass fear of loss is
emptied. does the moon care? the moon
does not give a flying fuck. the full
frost moon answers to no one. take
what persephone has. take from her
hand like a god – you afraid who.

THE WEEK-LATE ANSWER TO THAT
HOT-TEMPERED TEXT ON MY BIRTHDAY

beloved

yes, let's put it this way for nostalgia.
i would always answer right away
if i thought – write away
meant anything could find you
receptive not just receiving
like a criminal enjoys a prison stint
 – if matter were material
and could be tongued like a scream,
kissed like a fist,
bitten through
as a bottom lip in the fall,
or
snapped between teeth
as bacon is shattered meat.
but it doesn't matter, doesn't add up
 – weighs negative something.
why give credence to myth by prayer
or declare to the dead i am living?
i can't stand a ghost story
 – never got the point of haunting halls
over the care less of frightened fools.

In the top drawer of your heart
you keep all you closed.
Only at night do you allow
yourself permission to unfold hope
while the moon pulls
bright fingers through
your exhausted navy clouds.
What vows are appropriate
for the ceremony of desire
combing through your hair.
Even brutes temper strength
to clutch infant to chest
as cautious as physicians
palpate tender to
delineate wound.
He parts your hair
and pulls teeth gentle
through knots of trauma.
Each parting is hypnotic
each parting spell
and soothsay.
Creased into the form
of a crane you dream
of passage by rail
where you tongue blueberries
from palms trusted
not to hurt you.

The parting moon
is above the clouds
in front of tomorrow
like a cardinal folded away from summer
throws itself red against the snow
outside the window.

23.3.13

NOW I KNOW

Early September let sail and the magnolia that
dragged its resolve through another Canadian season
sported leaves swissed by the sempiternal hunger
of Japanese beetles.

Pay no mind. The holy life of leaves
dwindle. Instead, move eye to where
leaf joints slim branch, already next year's
publications swell there.

Magnolia shudders, as stars and saucers
of incense – a brilliance I'd been ignorant of
in Brooklyn, but now I knew.
Now I know,

the first cucumber on the vine needs to go
pronto or the vine hesitates to set more fruit.
That first loss wakes the whole heart to its task
sometimes forever.

To coax an apple tree, two years stingy,
back to its business of pome making, take
shovel to root across dripline; threaten
its lazy ass with return to New York.

Oh it will hop to apple-making quick-fast
next year. A thing can forget what it's made
to do, even a natural thing. Use verse to cleave
feed roots. Make it taste the salt of its mortality.

07.9.16

re: stacks

my love is a pair of shoes
there was need for,
bought in haste
down
an unrepeatable street
at the base of a mountain
along the bay of naples
on the coast of amalfi,
made of scarlet leather
with cheek-tender lining.
did i already mention haste?
they were my favourite;
the first time
i tried to say
amo le scarpe.
i gave them to you
(tho you can't wear them
because you've never
seen my mountain nor
walked down the
happiest moment of my life
all of which miss you now).
we two-stepped to bon iver,
we side-stepped the obvious,
and today i see them
on your back porch,
in the rain, not ruined,
they were sewn too well
for forget, but under

the downfall they are
requesting a change
of song.

MIDDLE-AGE CARTWHEEL

a breath and then   foot
hand   hand   foot   foot
this is all there is supposed to be
to that

in the coiled tyger of abdomen
i recall as an old lover
the catch and release of each
fish muscle's lust for momentum

how i loathe the moment
the happiness of life
pivots on the webbing of carpus
and unity of eight innocent bones

beneath the caged flutter of hope
fear blooms in the liver as a spear
where memory burns its fever
across the spoke of my body

recall adolescent liberty
reclaim ignorance
of invulnerability
well-aged i know
what every alcoholic smells
in the flight plan of a fifth

sprain break traction
crookedness for what remains
premonitions of rain
misery of physiotherapy
jeer and disgust of your children
astute view of the fool you are

all for now this aching love
this tumbled shaken hour
upend and recovery now   breath
foot   handoverhand   foot   foot
sky.

THE LOVERS QUARREL

so the sun said
& the stars salted fight
so the moon said
so weary
sadness filled the dawning.

dia-mond dia-mond dia-mond
stars chanted
sang
or mumbled ashamed.

(is it love)

the sun manages against her nature
a question mark
love?
(not again)
the sun manages.
(the stars never really cared.)

then the moon
(his smile broken in half)
with & without sun said,
there is no help for any of it.
these estrangements
arranging derangements
orbit forever.

the afternoon tore down the middle as if tuesday
were an old reader's digest piled at the dentist's
with a desired recipe for gumbo – firm hold applied
to the centre then rent from top to bottom like

a no-longer-loved love letter trembles in the junction
of thumb and forefinger into half then four exponentially
less and more until it is unlike itself to the point
iota blooms as confetti for mardi gras and rejoicing

tuesday's shock of hungry raccoon prudent to rinse
cubed sugar ends with this macular degenerate of a day
kills the centre or gives the thin kiss of pneumonia
that holds while you pull and pull what won't come.

SCENE V

I don't know how to stay tender with this much blood in my mouth.

emma tranter

1. Blood, salty and metallic, a two for one on the anti-tenderness metre.

2. Any cook will tell you salt will toughen meat if you're not careful.

3. Take red paint, splash an unsuspecting bystander's white shirt. (In short order you see the impossibility of sweet excuses under a fountain of liquid red.)

4. Even if you start your morning cauterizing the jagged tears in your throat with a mantra of: sugar sugar sugar, spring days, café au lait, honey, molasses, and impressionist paintings, by the first jostle on the metro, honk in bumper to bumper, jerk at the cash, your chin drips crimson.

5. Who can save me from my own violent vocabulary – to sing a sparrow's fluted loss that soothes your soul that's my soul. And yet, like a room set with guillotines let fly, my sighs rain
vermillion.

11.7.16

has there been a night in thousands
that has seen me sleep without you?

your bare branches hold the story
of where and how everything was lost;

what happened with relevance (you
make a face when i say this, or try

not to, murmuring *june the obscure*).
accuracy is the order not hyperbole;

i swear to you – by whom
i've tasted faith under the blue shine

of your open night (this you really don't
believe).

i am begging you. pay attention
to my tender mathematics (that can't lie

to your question mark begetting
question marks).

sweet jesus. (i'm filling in this survey
as fast as i can!) grapefruit and kumquat

tears pool in the sour rage of a throat
thirsty for sweetness. calculus is unforgiving

– the horror-relief over such proof
is intense. winter, there came a time ...

you weren't in my bed (like this
cold twist) but in me.

Silence is the seed to grow my desire – silence and luck.
A large body of water shares clear clean glaze whispers,
hydrogen bonding; its difficulty is holding stillness; that's not
the fate God gave it. Lake Michigan's azure nudity faces
forward, echoes difference and distances, says Eden.

Good morning, America. *Good Morning America* called
the Sleeping Bear Dunes the Most Beautiful Place in
America. Toward the top, a breeze hurting of milkweed
promises life after death. At apex, the landscape bursts
blue like a Black Southern woman shreds into tears.
I hear you suck teeth and curl Brooklyn snarl: You lie
like a dog. Man, I wouldn't do you like that.

Only lie-strung hyperbole twins absolute truth about blue sky
kissing belly of smooth lake hinting at forever,
what Miles Davis meant by great and grand. Who am I
to argue the heart's fatback thunder like Art Blakey rolled
Lee Morgan?

A frail woman places diamond over dust against warning
of falling rocks, or arduous journey back, to descend the gold
slope of sand – desire's end in rare pause and beauty's bite.

In the distant midst of turquoise impossibility,
a small white triangle was shouting something in Italian.
I answered that sail, *Mi dispiace! I do not speak your language!*
At that point, I regretted not knowing how to gnash teeth or
why the g is silent.

Years after, during a solo sail on Lake Champlain,
a port tack wind unfurled the mystery from Lake Michigan.
I come from the future! (I'd shouted in Spanish-accented
Italian.)

Don't let a present helplessness spoil any moment.
You learn to sail where coyotes howl to the loon's canto,
and the flight of horned owl burns September
on silent wing. I know you don't know
what I'm saying, but you will.

I'd envied the far white sail that afternoon (to the prick
of hatred like a knife in the neck); it hurt that someone else had
a silence of life as lapis and innocent as making love in a dream.

Drive a breeze. Act as propitiation between sail and wave.
Keep sacred the love for silence where whispering water slaps
attention along your hull granting sweet fortune
of how the wind can heel you.

hold a view
you on a chair febrile & thirsty;
from above he pours into the cup of your waiting
a glass sand memory.

grain, tumbled world, glint of cobalt, green
(celadon sea to forest deep), smoke, & troves
of gold – tyger-eye & beer bottle molasses.

the ocean overture frosts time
blunting all but diamond hurts
the tiniest bits fresh & sharp.

gather trust as a weapon against the past
– agile waves of cool clarifying tune –
counter to isolation in the swelter belly of summer.

your lover's years burst into the unobtainable
cosmos. dust in the glimmer gaze of entropy.

undimmed by jealousy's lighter than air smoke
you are determined
to land what teethes the line
even against the gravity of fear
in your power.
fear, what he undresses
                              like a physician grades
the take of a skin graft
                              over the scar of memory.

although you are two neodymium magnets
separated by the paper of the past
your arsonist heart shakes accelerants
over offering – a perverse mode of keeping

– awkward transfer to positive effect.

CONNECTIONS

a sneeze is also a sign of arousal
– the devil's foothold in a cold.

are you the answer to my dreams?
sunrise is a nightmare to the sunburned.

i feel like i have always loved you
– what a fool says.

close is our safest distance
– the medicine for silent indecency.

even when i lived next door,
i was never the girl next door.

i've fallen with my nose in the butter
– a lucky thing.

there is no mama bear chair in november;
inside is the only outside i can endure.

spell check changes hijab into human,
Angrignon to angry gringo – angling meal.

a gobble of turkeys watch the train
where i – like god – eat a turkey sandwich.

eagles fly high lazy loops of
what-looks-good-today?

cormorants race through the air as
furrowed brows.

men rule the world because women have to
keep brushing the hair out of our eyes.

i feel powerfully powerless once my hair
strokes my shoulders.

i never register make & model but know
under the navy velvet belly

of southern night there's not much
space between lap & steer wheel.

mahogany perfume soaks ivory hues
sugar takes its cues from me.

wall street's bull longs to take charge while
dixie anthems power crimson's liquid rise.

what hangs from them trees   moss?
strange twin to shred plastic bags

waving down fifth avenue's sycamores.
i cup your hand under peach blouse

when together brushes blackberry
we inhale bourbon strong your whisper

drawl slow a drawn bow upper hand
– seek in quiver the notes

ask coffee mirror water powerful words
that resound difference more than skin thrust.

hungry for peace kneeling in your heart
you say *strike* whisper *do what you desire*.

13.11.16

LOVE LIKE A WANING MOON

like salmon
mad for upriver
the way the monarch
is a milkweed junkie
strung out
cat's cradle
around
your fingertips.
this hunger is geese
with ironed
alphabet
in wings
making south
as an arrow of screams
cleaves
your sagittal plane
lodging near
your sweet fourth rib.
the same vacant haunt
of screech owl
head on backwards
eyes demented for scurry
tearing the blueberry night
apart.
sharp as the click
and swallow
of the word inexplicable
in the ocean's moans of
why moon why?

COME BACK AND SOLVE FOR X
Longing, we say, because desire is full of endless distances.

Robert Hass

somewhere inside stillness you move
        your thirsty hunger upsets time
am i solving for your happiness or mine
        it would help to settle the perimeter of beginning
it would help if we defined our variables
        who is the cause of our effect
come rest your atlas on my axis
        pivot on our common denominator
instead of this endless expanse of irrational numbers
        at the finish of this i want to line up x
to the third power with u and carry them and live there
        inside your y until the end of pi.

SOFT PART

open mouth
insert tongue
probe.

tooth tooth tooth
remove
the word love.

taste the el
on fire
the oh
full of
surprise.

vee is
serrated.
you taste
the flow
of your
own metal
anguish

viscous & crimson
as the bitter
it comes from.

pass back
the e to
me.

oh
you
who bare the soft part

of what i said.

06.10.15

A FIREFLY TURNS ON THE EVENING'S FIRST LIGHT

For our anniversary, instead of the love you want,
I wrap apology in silk and silent adoration,
which slips past you unmarked as you go about
cutting pancakes into soft acute angles with the absent
look of dreaming that I could be different or you could.

Lingering in the cool at the lip of the river
watching sunset then moonrise, the steady
move of the articulate earth painted the water hues
bold then very solemn. It seemed, at the hush,
when a firefly turns on the evening's first light, you
painted my face in the same expectation of grace.

A face I can no longer notice without seeing you
there or not there, just as the white line of pink moon
on the water nods toward the vanishing point. Who said,
you don't know your own language until you've learned
another? Did Goethe realize how much he knew about love?

How for your birthday, the day I would be born,
I tried to place my hand in the hollow made for it,
the hand that had not fit any stanza right until you.

04.4.16

gold circuits
on or off –
a fourteen karat
ring
of no decibels
slim
to a finger.

the glass-
scratching
precious is pear-cut
light broke
to rainbow glint
– centred & sided
by twin
blood-fire flanks
square & flesh-mounted
yellow closure.

the slim finger is
absent. the ring
signals nothing
holds less
in it or together.

a throat
a troth
an O.

first, a leopard frog triangles stillness whispering,
take ease, to the woman clearing her pool.

thirty minute spiral – brown algae vacuumed from perimeter
to drain in slow concentric ritual that churns mind not muck.

overhead, into every breeze, an army of lindens sneeze
pea-sized seed; she gathers – discards their myriad hope.

hose gone – the leopard frog hunts, oblivious to
the excited calypso vibrating from Dominican neighbours,

or circling helicopter (a mystery in this small town),
or the nth lawn mower's roar heightened there, there, and there.

a tiny fist of sun twitches at its feeder – a goldfinch
pitched loop-de-loop into blue fir stands. she counts:

breakfast and work, a letter to her sister, dishes,
and work. a few chapters of Al-Khalili made her think

of the false planetary model of electrons and what other
gross simplicity obscured the wake of true hours. frog,
copter, fist.

like a wave, she shimmers in and out of existence.
a grief of impermanence feeds longing for an anchoring gaze.

how does one become solid beyond any observation.
every hour she flows faster away from herself.

at this exact moment, unknown to her, someone she loved dies.
already the sun was sleepy-eyed, the illusion of time – laughter

adding another wrinkle, while the frog seems glued
in its faux cement planter under blue bells and thirsting

where it will be tomorrow when she, with hose and espresso,
carries a watermark gouging the groove of her tongue.

you buy a half-litre of cabernet sauvignon
for under twenty bucks & start tucking in
right away.

thoughts crash down the aisle like a late
november thunderstorm on the coldest day
of the year.

a year begun in ventricle-chilling fog. a sip
then he appears hooded-eye & sullen at the
front of the car.

you're already moist and disbelieving as he takes
your plastic Greenware cup: *cups from plants
make a difference.*

right there he starts to make a difference with
you on the floor between seats (the aisle
also implicated).

by god people will just have to step around.
his mouth closes over in an appeal
of serpent and vacuum seal.

you want to die in this torrent of melting. die
grabbing collar seeking continuance to
this poem.

which can't end! can't end here while so many
avert their eyes – not with this can't-be-happening
& always wanted.

always wanted your tygersoul gordian knotted
– an absolute wreck of unfettered imagination
& whet possibility.

PART FOR ME

gulf of mexico.
my knee is strongly against
the tide
of your refusal;
solar flares pizzazz
overcast skies
with a nudge
of insistent shine.
i hate to tell you
what comes next;
i hate to tell you
the hard look of helpless
splintering
across your horizon.
which i ignore
like your utterance of: callous.
don't you know?
your every look
is already engraved in me,
scripted along
the black of my right shoulder
you can read it in the dark
by light fingers
or the purple clouds of memory.
anyway, awareness
feeds some childhood terror.
childish
forgive me;
it can't be helped;

black skin burns blue
under the full moon;
salt and caramel
complement as do
chocolate and chilies.
do you think this is easy for me?
baby, it's a heartbreaker
coaxing spring from frozen soil;
i promise
i'm singing into your
puckered wound
as tenderly as i can (which
still seems to pink you).
part for me.
i stay
idling.
give in.
it's holding the ocean
back that aches;
it is the way
you don't want me
to say
what i'm going to say.

IN ANSWER TO MY I LOVE YOU

smoke signals

distant

and white

my teeth chatter

up this olive tree.

hasty facade constructed

with no *i*(s)

one could

one might

look

there

a dove with a broken

line.

in answer to my seems

hems, perforations, pain,

gestures of

away

brush my crumbs free

of your lap

wave

faded blanket over

black fire

i thought you were alive.

can there be smoke

without your body

you are already

down mount royal

silence unfolded

MAKE THE NEXT SECOND CHANCE

I dare to take my foundling hope as bone
& drop it in the turbulent rise of your body.
We paint white walls black joy after suffering
the dank chill of north's insistent wind.

By afternoon we defined away sadness
like a house unroofed its melancholy shingle
replacing grey's bitter cover with a glass pitch
that lets in what's crimson & molasses.

For kicks stalk Jupiter's gas oceans
then crawl to the mound again moth & moon
again crawl to pink mouth warm & song again
our moment held tongue & hand.

In an eye stippled with tumors every glance
is cancerous, a daguerreotype landscape
over-developed fading to white. We tremble
separated from the double bunk of past & forever.

Somnambulant in suburban dreams
we capstone guts tenderized under a symphony
of the bombastic fist of our fathers' wishes.
In the morning mother filled our cracks
full of gold
                blanket stitching with our tears
our solos together.

We swim through Venus' lavender rains
then crawl to the mound again moon & moth
again crawl to your salt mouth & song again
our moment held breath & horses.

We make a second chance against what
autumn removed. I dare to unzip your spring
sliding hand down the crevice of our soul.
Have faith it's only winter once a year.

NERVE DAMAGE

today, a grey squirrel, two weeks face down in the pool,
enjoys the ecosystem of whisper-thin linden leaves
that escaped the autumn raking to float, freeze, thaw,
and bleach, in spring sun, until they are ghosts.
moss-like algae speaks round the petal ears
of the petite brute's decay. two days before,
a flock of white-capped sparrows picked through
the field of front yard in a spirit of what could be called
hope. an unhinged squirrel kept running them off –
an annoyance and agony that everything is itself.

watering the stirring magnolia, i found one sparrow
dead by the water spout. the masculine golden feathers
still bright around his departed eyes.
i'd hurt myself sneezing, which made me remember
a fifteen-year-old girl who'd just had a baby boy.
she said, *i didn't get not one single tear!* for the briefest
sneeze we are invincible. if you fall asleep with your arm
over your head and manage dreaming in that position
after a few hours you will wake up with nerve damage.
i collapse into every rest like an open grave
the body wants to be there; the body floats toward eyeless
and the slim cover of a transparent fall.

IF WE ARE SAVAGE & LUCKY
for Lawson Fusao Inada

Where else could you be? Rulers and hearts broken.
What reverie descends, wet Saturday afternoon,
late October, parked on a floral-patterned
velvet chesterfield,
in front of a TV movie of World War II heroic.
When it began you groaned,
not World War II again, but there you were
watching American square jaws save the free world.
You search for your phantom tollbooth
between sobs of rain, internal commotion
knocks like unbalanced laundry,
impatient for an engineer to correct
pandemonium – askew horizon, no corner
a true right angle. The kisses the sand plum blows,
against the far window, remind you of shelter
once taken, under metal lean-to, by a river with *him*
heavy in your heart as wet sand. Now
would be the perfect moment
to plate his head in your lap. Let idle hands love
what they do while eyes feast war and ears harmonize
fallen music with a memory of steel drum.
If he were a mountain chain singular on top of you,
and not fragments like corporal Smithy
(recently blown to Hollywood *hambourgeois*),
you could search veiled eyes, knead smooth
knotted anxiety, sample saltsweet tongue,
pour gin and beer kiss; explain to him definitively
broken things are often replaced, and what has fallen
crooked with abuse may be shored-the-fuck-up

– winched back into place. *This rain* you say out loud
in a mania of gestures against an aria of cannons,
it's still my favourite. Still yours.

i'm afraid of owning a rabbit,
afraid of startled-to-death
or watching a local red-tail
soar off with its easy sandwich.

i'm trying to evade
the love that stakes me.

when we meet, you will say, ...

then i laugh, responding,
don't fall in love with me,
because we have *too late,*
like tragedy forming marrow,
metastasizing in bone.

someone said:
sunrise is a nightmare to the sunburned.
brown don't burn in the sun.
sugar, do you?

this morning i ate oysters, eggs,
and the last bit of cake,
flaunting my alpha predator state.

was i the only one who
stepped on cracks
hoping to break my mother's back?

we do what we can
and if we hunt lucky
we do what we can't.

11.11.17

VISION

she asked
      or he asked

                once
      out of concern (or was it curiosity?)

doesn't having visions mean you're cracking up?

she
      or he
            was sitting on the remaining cross-section
                    of felled cottonwood.
we were drinking gin.
            (or vodka)
trying to forget
how old we were yet to be.
          i still couldn't tell him how often
i'd seen myself kiss your fingertips
        at the most inopportune
            moments
– that time your hands were earth-covered
and your back
       wore a salt slick of hard labour
           while your mouth dispensed
           a molasses of cursing
        the worksong moving you through
          hated and necessary

            to the return of the ocean shush
                of your solitude
    your god-work she whispers *sotto voce*
            as this work whispers
            and wants your tips
        (like california's frogs croak: *water*)
        just when you most want yourself
                for yourself,

and also during fights
                over some bright bird
                                of stupidity
                                        that

            (at the time)

seemed worth the hullabaloo of tangerine
                and ochre flap
a parrot spooked off perch
                        – in a heat over fears neither of us
                            have the stones to name.
even if your heart
                knocks everything off the table
                    or your
i'm-heading-north thumbs
                worry the wear in the knee of your jeans
                                    i want a taste.
you'd think disappointment unlikely salt
                            to thirst for prints
with lips and tongue but somehow yes.

            and what is fiction finally

but the clear seeing of what isn't there.

                                    what's not yet.

i'm cracking

                for sure

                      but solid by line pull to tip.

THE WALL
for LG

he wasn't drunk yet,
but he had whisky & directions.
said, *i called her a cunt*;
told her,
i hope he breaks
your heart.

a child tells their father,
i hate you & means it
with the roiling
impotent venom
only the purest love conjures.

livid tendrils
of helpless vined him
as that Asian tree in Brooklyn
under the slimmest eyelid of earth
worms its way to foothold
then sprints its one mad life
his full six feet. rage
unpeeled suffering eclipsed
the jade afternoon
shadowed our empty bowls.
i pressed myself on top of her
(finally arrived at skunk)
her shirt buttons dug in
while she looked through me
like a window
 – cataclysm of
electric indifference.

what seared me years after
was my secret betrayal.
i watched him flamed
and what lilted through my head
as blood-parched fantasy was
this music of hurt was beauty
 – summit to be gained.
i'd no idea
how high my love stood;
i never lost my head
trying to see
over the wall of you.

REASONABLE AMOUNT OF TENDERNESS
When people show you who they are, believe them.

Maya Angelou

it's important to avoid hyperbole
grant each wish lungs to breathe. fact,
I spout lava when I ought to blow pensive.

it's one thing to say, when someone
shows you who they are believe them,
it's another to swallow that dry lump.

I overlaid hope with a rose-tone you,
but now I step into sunset seep into

a clear glass of corn whisky;
surrender to the general of grief.

respect alive;
pray to what immolates you.

a lost grip means love with open palms,
and wisdom quenches people burning as bridges.

addict forever to fire and flood,
more dreamer than awake – hugging every impossible
tree with embarrassing conviction.

you offered, as sly, the knife of white winter,
and I still saw you as more beautiful than you saw
yourself; for this, you will never forgive me.

I wanted *you-present*
and I would've signed with *you-future*
but I can't love you from before I was.

the sutured soul is dying
for reasonable tenderness.

you raised a glass to my all-seeing-eyes – that now
laser through you – accepts your no of no answer.

OF COURSE THIS BRICK

of form & function
is a type of marriage
just not the one wanted
corner of a church
traverse the pane
possibility
hold the closed door open.

23.1.17

as a finger of pulled cotton, the white root splits the hardness
of sleeping seed.

fine fibres sate the head's thirsty stem. songs of tenderness
break earth's hidden hunger.

come autumn tired vines tangle into spider
toughness and refusal is the cadaver of spent dream

like the small boy after first strike of electric anger
(as if virtue could be waved in on palms of rage).

he swears to *never-ever* be worthy of the bruise,
disappointment; he folds softness like geography inside a fist,

boxes tender, boxes it and forgets where
 – till forty when his wife escapes his hideous closure.

wound and knotted round the purpling night sky he finds
his hid thing – a round belt of silvering stars.

how little brash men consider June women opening
and the necessity of parting, as carefully as possible, the hull.

true, the nature of a rose is thorned (though a few haven't any
while some emerge as barbed wire) still

every thorn is red-born and bendable. they say, *careful*, in
husked tones, not, *stay away*.

love, gather colours loosed in the brute hot of masculine July.
say what is beautiful; bring her re-bloom that wakes come June.

CIRCLE EARTH: MEDITATION AFTER
READING TROPIC OF CANCER

the loose-toothed man
with a ming-blue eye visible
behind shades with one lens
pedals a tricycle burdened
with bottles and dry coke cans

you imagine henry valentine's
face sagging like a man's shoe
under bald head with his wit for words
mutter *look at all them cunts*
you mutter back *indeed*
like the coward you are

you mean hero
hero of the uncommitted
your weak knees are hereditary
you test a little jump of gratitude
for the heights you can still attain
never one who failed to quit while behind

when the tricyclist passes the fourth time
you are firmly irritated; is he waiting for you
to put down this can of cream soda?
a girl whizzes by atop a gold two-wheeler
her serious face a polished piano
her black sphere of hair clears a sun path
she is being perfectly

beauty berates cynicism forty-nine times
with an ax
she effortlessly holds up the universe.

CANADIAN GOOSE SUMMER

do you recall hibiscus winter
blooms coral with pause not déjà vu memory?

its twin volcano belched feathers and envy.
do you recall your partiality – a gold ring erased

that circled my passion before you took it back.
i was taken aback. hurt, not by the november

of meeting but by the blunt force of autumn fear.
why harbour craven as diaphanous hours

or nurse with nectar the coward who betrays you?
throbbing unhoused as feral goddess,

sitting skirt and pant leg abreast on august
porch swing. alone, shared memory inflicts

corporal punishment. sun's cold shoulder.
moon's white-gold, loose-tooth grin.

want burned whisky-eyed and tygerish
against a south hewn in ice.

ONE TWO THREE TOUCH OR HOW NOT
TO DANCE THE BACHATA

One two three touch.
This, the simple code from hip to floor
to the trills of the tiny guitar of Rafael,
but code eludes him.

Two take dance classes instead of therapy,
putting in the work – hard at
the tattered seam of one garment stitched
in cloths of differing weights.

Three lurch
opposing the sanctity of dance,
his hip-to-ankle seemingly fused
to invisible two-by-four;
they shuffle as a grotesque marionette
as *la maestra* Josée shadows him
trying from behind
to crease Welsh knees in correct rhythm.

Touch.
Bliss has need for too many bends
– hope-toned, farcical,
a commitment to commitment
tries to conjure magic on beat.
No shame when they finally land
the lesson, cry *Tío*, admit wishing
won't partner what can't be felt.

WITH SOFT EYES SHE LEARNED TO SEE
THE CURVATURES OF SPACETIME
IN THE OMNIPRESENT GRID OF HOPE
AND THEN CRY ACCORDINGLY
Chaos is a ladder.

Petyr Baelish, *Game of Thrones*

It was awful – being unable to give up, aching for
rewards from pessimism rather than idealism's scourge
and scars. Working her way up to breakdown,
she learned to orgasm silently – let hope pass
like a tarantula might cross your foot on its way
to a tea party.

For no reason, or for whatever reason long forgotten,
gold-plated carelessness broke something in her
 – delicate had been the purl stitch pulling together.

A full jar of peanut butter and knife
grace a cupboard without a lick of bread.
She clears her throat to scat – broadcasting
Mayday, Juneday, Julyday to the moon's stoic receiver.

Who wanted the apology for what she'd done?
Tell evening she had regrets (for trusting),
but she couldn't lie, not so bald – couldn't catch
life through denial of what was most caught.

Love wasn't made for her, but she, sure as hell,
was made for it, like a donut grabs its hole,
marries coffee, tastes best on the first day.
The pressure for useful was tsunamic aphrodisiac.

In Alabama, Señora García pauses at the blackboard, then sneezes; in Brooklyn, an entire class catches cold.

In an average lifespan a person invests a year looking for the things they've forgotten.

9 august 2017

Those who have laboured, night and day, Monday to Friday, on their unhappiness are right to lick their chops over it as much as they do.

11 august 2017

In the contorted bookkeeping of the broken, the distance you hold yourself away from them is your only value.

12 august 2017

TFW YOU WANT TO FUCK WITH THEM FROM NOW UP INTO FOREVER, but all signs and wonders, Urim and Thummim, emails and texts, no email, no texts, using the good-got-damn-sense your mother gave you, not repeating the mistakes your father braided, tell you to keep things cute and quick. ¡Presta atencíon!

No exit interview no two weeks notice.

Numbers 31:19
Anyone who has killed any person or touched the slain must stay outside the camp seven days. Clean yourself and your captives.

did you clean yourself
you who has touched
who has violated my pen
has salted my tongue
drugged my drink
slain with the blade
of lack of empathy

a ladder like love leans
outside of time
goes up and down
through the same insistence

Easier to be angry than afraid, easier to brace guilt rather
than test sick with intimate.

1. i'm easily disgusted while others have more robust guts
2. i need to know who died so i can know how sad i should be
3. i'm trying to say the world opens on the jagged
4. we're romantic about loneliness or melancholia, when we need to be pragmatic – use blueprints to build across not behind
5. there are people capable of eating popcorn at the movie of your agony; do not marry him or him (note to my younger self)
6. cool intimacy – like making love in silence – like watching porn with the sound off (which is preferable)
7. our suspended disbelief becomes a marionette we wield: GODLIKE
8. at times, life seems to be writing syntactically correct nonsense
9. poets lie definitively – it's exhausting – salmon go up and shit floats down; poetry then no refuge from the deluge
10. (note to self: move up river)
11. memory is warmth in the sheets after the body leaves
12. there are always infinite excellent tenets for being a coward
13. on the plastic torture chairs in emergency, over loudspeakers in french and english bubbles, they warned one of us to get out – in my best edward g. robinson public address system diction i whispered *Paging Doctor Garbles to Linguistics*

14. (tormented) now that you've left me for her in albuquerque, i'm a wraith rattling disjointed and hostile along the rio grand, scaring strangers that pass in and out of me, looking like your sons. this, i don't mind. not the way, these nipples miss your lips and ache for articulation. infuriated, the reader knocks at the door (like all hell) *let me in!* in terror, i am sharpening a meat cleaver, shouting at the window, *i haven't got a key!* one crystal moment, you came to the cradle of my arms, the fragrant and hearty imperial stout of thirty-year-melancholy and the disaster of aggressively avoiding a bright fate that now you seek down down river, far from the soft ghost that loved you somewhere in the stanzas of new mexico.

OVERCAST

you've tasted the soup
of scorched tomato and broccoli
that set your teeth on edge
but you've not met that loss
that permanently skews
the jaw
grief that plants
sunset in the eye forever
remember the high-spirited mum
with a quick and rainbow smile
whose daughter died at nine
many decades ago
she carries that weather
like an open umbrella
bills got paid
lovers found
and lost found
and lost and lost
but it stayed
it stays
a reason for it makes you believe
in god
it makes you hate it
– your belief.

"People Believing Badly" was a *Verse Daily* Web Weekly
Feature, and has been translated into Farsi in *Persian Sugar
in English Tea*, vol. 3, by editor: Soodabeh Saeidnia

"ALLIIALLOWMAS"
Jean M. Twenge, "Have Smartphones Destroyed a
Generation?" *The Atlantic*, September 2017

"Boots of Spanish Leather"
is a song written by Bob Dylan from his *The Times They
Are a-Changin'* album (1964)

"Catching Sight of The Niña The Pinta & The Santa Maria"
title borrows a phrase from "In Memory of My Feelings"
by Frank O' Hara

"Tinder of the 'Desperate Man'"
the author's translation of:
... it is a characteristic of wisdom not to do desperate things.
– Henry David Thoreau

"THE PHYSICS OF LOVE AND OTHER UNCERTAIN
PHASES OF THE CHEMISTRY IN COULOMB'S LAW"
section III. references Italian physicist Carlo Rovelli who
writes wonderful compact books for laypeople on physics

"I/U"
is read: I divided by U or I over U is permissible but not I
slash U

"Now I Know"
it's true you can sometimes coax a fruit tree that has stopped setting fruit to bloom the following spring by cutting a circle in the soil with a shovel in the autumn

"re: stacks"
alludes to the Bon Iver song of the same name and spelling

"Scene V"
the epigraph, by the poet emma tranter [sic], from her *heartless girls zine*, is often misattributed on the social media network Tumblr to Ophelia in Hamlet, Scene V. emma tranter AKA *fairytalephoenix.tumblr,* AKA *asombregirl.tumblr*

"How the Wind Heels You"
heel is a sailing term to describe the leaning of the vessel

"Connections"
the author is aware that a group of turkeys is not called a gobble

"Love Like a Waning Moon" was translated into Farsi in *Persian Sugar in English Tea*, vol. 3, by editor: Soodabeh Saeidnia

"Twenty-Four Hours in the Life of a Frog" references British physicist Jim Al-Khalili, author of *Quantum: A Guide for the Perplexed* (Orion Publishing Group, 2012)

"OMFG: UNTIL THE TYGER LEARNS HOW TO WRITE"
Numbers 31:19 is the author's own translation using an amalgamation of other interpretations and doesn't duplicate any translation known to the author

"WITH SOFT EYES SHE LEARNED TO SEE THE
CURVATURES OF SPACE TIME IN THE OMNIPRESENT
GRID OF HOPE AND THEN CRY ACCORDINGLY"
epigraph is from the episode "The Climb" (season 3,
episode 6), on the television show *Game of Thrones*, written
by David Benioff and D.B. Weiss.

"Overcast"
also included in the League of Canadian Poets' Poetry Pause
and first prize in *The Sixty Four: Best Poets 2018*
(Black Mountain Press)

ACKNOWLEDGMENTS

Deepest gratitude to The Doll, Melanie, Deidre, and Whit Schweizer for the years of caring. Thanks to all of the McGill-Queen's University Press team for their support of this collection. Thank you to Mark Abley, who initially followed my work, and editor Allan Hepburn, whose gentle guidance led to the finish.

The author gratefully acknowledges the publishers and editors of the journals in which the following poems first appeared (sometimes with slight alteration):

"People Believing Badly," *Blue Lyra Review*
"TEMPESTA: TUESDAY DECEMBER TWENTIETH THREE THREE THREE AY EM," *The Ocotillo Review*
"The Woods of Perhaps," *River Heron Review*
"Forest Nocturne," *The Write Launch*
"Passages North," "Make the Next Second Chance," *Canada Quarterly*
"Father Son Spirit," "Tinder of the 'Desperate Man,'"
"How the Wind Heels You," *Burning House Press*
"This Is About Being Black," *The New Quarterly*
"Boots of Spanish Leather" previously known as "Because," *Gaze*
"THE OPENING LITURGY OF THE MORNING'S FIRST DRAFT IS ALL FUCKING WHILE THE EVENING MAKES LOVE AS THE GOOD POET PUTS IT," *Breakwater Review*
"i never tire of the moon," *Crannóg Magazine* (Pushcart Prize nomination)
"Set Fire to Stop Fire," *Goat's Milk Magazine*

"Something Terrible Is Going to Happen," "re: stacks,"
"Come Back and Solve for x," *bloodsugarpoetry*
"Catching Sight of The Niña The Pinta & The Santa Maria,"
The Maine Review
"Off Hours," *Rising Phoenix Review*
"Commute the Sentence," "Canadian Goose Summer,"
L'Éphémère Review
"THE PHYSICS OF LOVE AND OTHER UNCERTAIN
PHASES OF THE CHEMISTRY IN COULOMB'S LAW,"
The Gambler
"Tame," *Waxing & Waning*
"THE WEEK-LATE ANSWER TO THAT HOT-TEMPERED
TEXT ON MY BIRTHDAY," *The Indianapolis Review*
"I/U," *A Velvet Giant*
"Now I Know," *Before After/Godwink*
"Middle-Age Cartwheel," *Bacopa Literary Review*
"The Lovers Quarrel," *Priestess & Hierophant Press*
"Slim Tuesday," "No Such Forever," *Occulum Journal*
"Scene V," "Love Like a Waning Moon," *Claudius Speaks*
"Hold Desire as Sand," *The Slag Review*
"Connections," "If We Are Savage & Lucky," "If We Are
Savage & Lucky II," "Overcast," *Banshee*
"Black Lashes & White Pickup Accents," *Juke Joint*
"Soft Part," *After the Pause*
"A Firefly Turns on the Evening's First Light," *Reunion:
The Dallas Review*
"Twenty-Four Hours in the Life of a Frog," *Two Chairs Poetry*
"Via Rail Dreaming," *Subterranean Blue Poetry*
"Part for Me," *Gyroscope Review*
"Nerve Damage," *JARFLY Magazine*
"Vision," *EVENT Magazine*
"Of Course This Brick," *River River*

"CIRCLE EARTH: MEDITATION AFTER READING TROPIC OF CANCER," *The Stockholm Review of Literature*
"WITH SOFT EYES SHE LEARNED TO SEE THE CURVATURES OF SPACETIME IN THE OMNIPRESENT GRID OF HOPE AND THEN CRY ACCORDINGLY," *Emrys Journal*, www.emrys.org
"OMFG: UNTIL THE TYGER LEARNS HOW TO WRITE," *Brain Mill Press*
"Rushes from the River Disappointment," *Arcturus*